# ST. LOUIS

# CARDINALS

## BY PATRICK DONNELLY

SportsZone

An Imprint of Abdo Publishing
abdobooks.com

abdobooks.com

Published by Abdo Publishing, a division of ABDO, PO Box 398166, Minneapolis, Minnesota 55439. Copyright © 2023 by Abdo Consulting Group, Inc. International copyrights reserved in all countries. No part of this book may be reproduced in any form without written permission from the publisher. SportsZone™ is a trademark and logo of Abdo Publishing.

Printed in China.
102022
012023

Cover Photo: John Fisher/Getty Images Sport/Getty Images
Interior Photos: Jeff Roberson/AP Images, 4; Chicago Sun Times/Chicago Daily News collection/Chicago History Museum/Archive Photos/Getty Images, 7; The Stanley Weston Archive/Archive Photos/Getty Images, 9; George Rinhart/Corbis Historical/Getty Images, 11; AP Images, 12, 15, 20; Bettmann/Getty Images, 16, 19, 21, 25; Focus on Sport/Getty Images, 22, 26, 31; Larry Lambrecht/Major League Baseball/Getty Images, 28; James A. Finley/AP Images, 32; Jed Jacobsohn/Allsport/Getty Images Sport/Getty Images, 35; Mike Simons/AP Images, 37; Eric Gay/AP Images, 39; Joe Robbins/Icon Sportswire/AP Images, 41

Editor: Charlie Beattie
Series Designer: Becky Daum

**Library of Congress Control Number: 2022940481**

**Publisher's Cataloging-in-Publication Data**

Names: Donnelly, Patrick, author.
Title: St. Louis Cardinals / by Patrick Donnelly
Description: Minneapolis, Minnesota: Abdo Publishing, 2023 | Series: Inside MLB | Includes online resources and index.
Identifiers: ISBN 9781098290337 (lib. bdg.) | ISBN 9781098275532 (ebook)
Subjects: LCSH: St. Louis Cardinals (Baseball team)--Juvenile literature. | Baseball teams--Juvenile literature. | Professional sports--Juvenile literature. | Sports franchises--Juvenile literature. | Major League Baseball (Organization)--Juvenile literature.
Classification: DDC 796.35764--dc23

# CONTENTS

# CHAPTER 1

# CREATING THE CARDINALS

On Opening Day of the 2022 season, the St. Louis Cardinals' public address announcer began introducing the team's roster. Once he had read through most of the names, he came to one of the team's veterans. After listing a few of the amazing awards and statistics from the player's long career, the announcer finally said, "Ladies and gentlemen, welcome back to St. Louis, in a Cardinals uniform where he belongs, Albert Pujols!"

Pujols greeted his teammates, as well as the former Cardinals greats who had gathered for the big event. It was a welcome sight for Cardinals fans. Pujols, one of the greatest players in team history, had spent 11 years in St. Louis. He was

Albert Pujols acknowledges the crowd in St. Louis before his first at-bat of the 2022 season.

the National League (NL) Rookie of the Year in 2001. He then won three NL Most Valuable Player (MVP) Awards as a Cardinal. But he left as a free agent after the 2011 season to sign with the Los Angeles Angels.

Now, at 42 years old, he knew he didn't have much time left in his career. He also knew he wanted to finish where he started. In March 2022, he had signed a one-year contract with the Cardinals.

The fans let him know their feelings as he jogged onto the field. They gave him a long and loud standing ovation. They did the same thing when he came up to bat for the first time. He later admitted his emotions were close to the surface during his homecoming.



"I was trying to hold it in a little bit," Pujols said. "These fans really appreciate what I've done for this organization and hopefully I can continue to do that and finish strong."

## GOING BACK

Pujols is just one of many outstanding players who have worn a Cardinals uniform over the years. The team traces its roots back to 1882, when a team called the St. Louis Brown Stockings began playing in the American Association (AA). They shortened the name to Browns the next year and spent 10 seasons in the AA, winning four pennants.

Cardinals left fielder Jesse Burkett led the NL with a .376 batting average and 226 base hits in 1901.

The AA folded, so the Browns joined the NL in 1892. It was a rough start in the new league for the team. The Browns finished among the bottom three teams in the standings in six of their first seven NL seasons.

New ownership took over in 1899 and changed the team's nickname to the Perfectos. That lasted just one season before the Cardinals name was adopted for good. Team owners Frank and Stanley Robison also owned the NL's Cleveland Spiders. When they purchased the St. Louis franchise, the Robisons moved the Spiders' best players to their new club. That included future Hall-of-Famers Cy Young, Jesse Burkett, and Bobby Wallace. The Spiders flopped, losing a record 134 games. That caused the NL to fold the team and send the rest of its players to St. Louis for the 1900 season.

Unfortunately for the Cardinals, they were on the wrong end of a different talent raid in 1901. The American League (AL) declared itself a major league in competition with the NL that year. Many NL players were lured to the new league with its promise of higher pay. Young and Burkett were among the Cardinals who jumped over to the AL. Worse yet, the AL put one of its teams in St. Louis and named it the Browns. Now the Cardinals were in danger of losing both players and fans.

It didn't help attendance that the product on the field was so weak. From 1902 to 1920, the Cardinals finished above fifth place in the eight-team NL only twice. But in that period, St. Louis witnessed the debut of one of the greatest hitters in Major League Baseball (MLB) history.

## HERE COMES HORNSBY

Late in the 1915 season, a skinny 19-year-old infielder named Rogers Hornsby joined the Cardinals. He struggled that year, but went home and added 30 pounds of muscle working on his family farm. The next year he was a starter. In 1920 Hornsby began one of the greatest hitting stretches in baseball history.

The second baseman led the NL in batting average, on-base percentage, and slugging percentage every year for six straight seasons. He hit .397 during that stretch. That included a .424 average in 1924. That remains the highest average the league

**Rogers Hornsby hit at least .370 every year from 1920 to 1925 and topped .400 three times.**

has seen since 1900. Hornsby took advantage of the huge outfields that ballparks had in that era to pile up doubles and triples. But he also led the majors in home runs and runs batted in (RBIs) in 1922 and 1925, giving him the NL Triple Crown in each of those seasons.

# BRANCH RICKEY

Cardinals general manager Branch Rickey was one of the most innovative figures in baseball history. Among other ideas, he is credited with inventing the modern farm system. He bought a series of minor league teams where the Cardinals' young players could gain experience. When his Cardinals teams had success with a wave of homegrown talent, other teams copied Rickey's model.

With Hornsby smashing baseballs, the Cardinals finally became a winning team. They got even better when the superstar became the team's manager. Hornsby took over when Branch Rickey moved to the general manager's position in 1925.

## CITY OF CHAMPIONS

A year later, the Cardinals put together a high-powered lineup that scored the most runs and hit the most home runs in the NL. Hall of Fame first baseman Jim Bottomley led the league with 40 doubles and 120 RBIs. Third baseman Les Bell hit .325 and drove in 100 runs. Hornsby remained a threat at the plate, despite focusing more on managing the team.

The team also brought in 39-year-old pitcher Grover Cleveland Alexander during the season. The former superstar was considered washed up in 1926, but Rickey took a chance. Alexander won nine games down the stretch, and the Cardinals won the NL on the way to their first World Series.

They faced the New York Yankees, whose legendary lineup was led by Babe Ruth and Lou Gehrig. Alexander came up big again, winning Games 2 and 6 in Yankee Stadium.

The Cardinals held a 3–2 lead in Game 7 when Alexander came out of the bullpen. The Yankees had the bases loaded with two outs in the bottom of the seventh inning. Once again, Alexander delivered, striking out New York's Tony Lazzeri to end the inning. Over the last two innings, the only base runner Alexander allowed was a two-out walk to Ruth in the ninth. However, the Yankees' slugger was caught stealing to end the game, giving St. Louis a thrilling World Series title.

**Grover Cleveland Alexander won 55 games for St. Louis over four seasons.**

# CHAPTER 2

# THE GASHOUSE GANG

After the 1926 World Series, Branch Rickey made a shocking move. Rogers Hornsby had been asking team owner Sam Breadon for more money. Breadon didn't want to budge. Instead, Rickey traded Hornsby to the New York Giants for second baseman Frankie Frisch.

The swap of future Hall of Famers began a transformation of the Cardinals' roster. Frisch was the first member of a group that would become known as "the Gashouse Gang." They were known for their scrappy, aggressive play. It was a style that gave them dirty uniforms that were often compared to an auto mechanic's grease-stained clothing.

After playing his college baseball at New York's Fordham University, Frankie Frisch earned the nickname "the Fordham Flash" for his speed.

Starting in 1928, the Cardinals won four of the next seven NL pennants. They lost the World Series to the New York Yankees in 1928 and the Philadelphia Athletics in 1930. A year later, the Cardinals and A's met again. Frisch led the way back to the Fall Classic by winning NL MVP.

The series went the distance. Rookie center fielder Pepper Martin made a big splash, batting .500 with 12 hits and five stolen bases. Game 7 took place in St. Louis's Sportsman's Park. The Cardinals took a 4–0 lead into the ninth inning behind the pitching of Hall of Famer Burleigh Grimes. But Grimes was tiring. The Athletics scored twice and had the tying runs on base. St. Louis's Bill Hallahan came out of the bullpen to get the final out and clinch the championship.

By 1934 the full Gashouse Gang had arrived in St. Louis. It included Martin, outfielder Joe "Ducky" Medwick, first baseman Ripper Collins, shortstop Leo Durocher, and Frisch at second base. But the two biggest stars were a pair of starting pitchers who happened to be brothers.

## DIZZY AND DAFFY

Jay Hanna Dean was signed away from a semipro team by the Cardinals in 1930. A full-time major leaguer two years later, he was a hit both on and off the field. The boisterous Dean never stopped talking. Martin once said that every game Dean

Brothers Paul "Daffy" Dean, *left*, and Jay "Dizzy" Dean were the Cardinals' ace pitchers during the early 1930s.

pitched "was like a three-ring circus and everybody was wide awake and enjoying being alive." Dean quickly earned the nickname "Dizzy" from the press.

In 1934 his brother Paul joined the Cardinals' rotation. The media quickly dubbed him "Daffy." The quieter Paul didn't like his new nickname, but it stuck. Meanwhile, Dizzy kept up his usual chatter. He boasted that Paul would win 18 to 20

**Outfielder Joe "Ducky" Medwick hit .379 in the 1934 World Series with a home run and five RBIs.**

games that year while Dizzy would win 20 to 25. They easily backed the statement up. Paul won 19, including a no-hitter in September. It came in the second game of a doubleheader. Dizzy had pitched a shutout in the first game. Afterward, the older Dean joked, "Shucks, Paul, you shoulda told me you was gonna pitch a no-hitter, then I woulda pitched one too!"

Dizzy more than held up his end of the bargain with 30 wins. And when the Cardinals needed to win their final series of the year to catch the first-place Giants, the Dean brothers came through. The pair won all three games to clinch the NL pennant.

## BRING ON DETROIT

In the World Series, the Cardinals faced the AL champion Detroit Tigers. Although the Cardinals took Game 1, the Tigers took three of the next four. The series shifted to Detroit for Game 6, but Paul Dean came to the rescue. He pitched a complete game and singled in the winning run in the seventh inning as St. Louis won 4–3.

Before Game 7, Dizzy spotted Tigers slugger Hank Greenberg on the field. "Boy, you're shakin' like a leaf," Dean reportedly said. "I get it; you done hear that Ol' Diz was gonna pitch. Well, you're right. It'll all be over in a few minutes."

Once again Dizzy backed up his talk. He tossed a shutout. And he also started a seven-run outburst in the third inning with a one-out double. Dizzy later scored on Frisch's bases-loaded triple as the Cardinals won 11–0. The Dean brothers had each won two games to bring home a third World Series title to St. Louis.

That was the peak for the Deans and the Gashouse Gang. Paul won 19 games again in 1935 before arm injuries derailed his career. Dizzy led the majors with 28 wins in 1935 and won

## MOTOR CITY RUMBLE

A brawl nearly broke out between the Cardinals and Detroit Tigers during Game 7 of the 1934 World Series. In the sixth inning, Joe Medwick hit a triple and slid hard into Detroit third baseman Marv Owen. The two had to be separated before a fight broke out. When Medwick went to play left field in the next half inning, Tigers fans pelted him with fruit and garbage. MLB commissioner Kenesaw Mountain Landis ordered the umpires to remove Medwick from the game for his own safety.

his fourth straight strikeout crown. But he broke his toe in the 1937 All-Star Game, tried to come back too soon, and injured his arm as a result. Other Gashouse Gang stars began to leave the team. But the Cardinals soon brought in one of the biggest heroes in team history.

## THE MAN

Stan Musial hoped to make it to St. Louis as a left-handed pitcher, but he injured his shoulder in the minor leagues. He switched to the outfield and showed he had plenty of talent as a hitter. Musial hit .315 as a rookie in 1942. That year the Cardinals won a franchise-record 106 games and took down the Yankees 4–1 in the World Series. Musial won the first of his seven NL batting crowns the next season, hitting .357.

Musial was a key figure as St. Louis won four NL pennants between 1942 and 1946. His left-handed batting stance looked odd. He bent his right knee and cork-screwed his body away from the mound as he waited for the pitch. But he sprayed line drives all over the field while leading the NL in doubles eight times and triples five times.

After losing to the Yankees in the 1943 World Series, the Cardinals faced the Browns in 1944 in the only all–St. Louis Fall Classic. Both teams were missing players to military service, but Musial and catcher Walker Cooper led the Cardinals to the

Stan Musial played in 24 All-Star Games over the course of his career, which is tied for an MLB record with Hank Aaron and Willie Mays.

title in six games. Musial spent the 1945 season serving in the US Navy, but he returned to help the Cardinals win another pennant in 1946.

Then, in an epic World Series against the Boston Red Sox, two more war heroes teamed up on the series' biggest play. Cardinals outfielders Enos "Country" Slaughter and Harry

Enos Slaughter slides home with the winning run in Game 7 of the 1946 World Series.

Walker also had returned from military duty in 1946. In Game 7 against Boston, the score was tied 3–3 in the bottom of the eighth. Slaughter led off with a single. Then, two outs later, he raced around the bases on Walker's double. Red Sox shortstop Johnny Pesky hesitated before making the relay throw to home plate, and Slaughter scored all the way from first. Slaughter's "Mad Dash," as it came to be known, gave the Cardinals a 4–3 win and another World Series title.

**Musial speaks to the St. Louis crowd at his retirement ceremony on the final day of the 1963 season.**

Musial's greatness continued as well. He won his third MVP Award in 1948 after he hit a career-high .376. He also came up one home run shy of the Triple Crown. He remained one of the game's top hitters in the 1950s and retired in 1963 with an NL-record 3,630 hits. Stan the Man never made it back to the World Series. But just as he was heading out, a new group of Cardinals was about to get St. Louis back on top.

# POWER AND SPEED

Bob Gibson was one of the most intimidating pitchers of the 1960s. He would stand on the mound with his hat pulled low, staring down hitters. The sight let batters know they were in for a rough time. Even worse, Gibson wasn't afraid to pitch inside. If a hitter crowded the plate, he soon felt one of Gibson's fastballs breeze past his head or slam into his thigh. Gibson was so intense, he wasn't even friendly with opposing players at the All-Star Game.

Gibson joined the Cardinals in 1959. By 1963 he was an 18-game winner, and the Cardinals' roster was starting to take shape. All four infielders—first baseman Bill White, second baseman Julián Javier, shortstop Dick Groat, and third baseman

Bob Gibson holds several St. Louis pitching records, including wins (251), complete games (255), and strikeouts (3,117).

Ken Boyer—made the All-Star team. The Cardinals won 93 games but came up just short of the World Series in Stan Musial's final season.

Musial's replacement was the speedy Lou Brock. The Cardinals picked up Brock in a 1964 midseason trade with the Chicago Cubs, and he made an instant impact. Brock hit .348 and stole 33 bases in just 103 games with St. Louis. Meanwhile, Boyer led the majors with 119 RBIs and was voted NL MVP. White, Groat, and center fielder Curt Flood also had All-Star seasons.

With Musial gone, the 28-year-old Gibson stepped up as one of the team's leaders on and off the field. At the time, racial tensions were rising in the United States. The Cardinals had a very diverse clubhouse, and Gibson and his Black teammates—especially Flood and White—were credited with keeping the team together. Often that meant challenging their white teammates who carried racial prejudice to change. All-Star catcher Tim McCarver credited Gibson with helping McCarver become more understanding. The two longtime teammates eventually built a lasting friendship.

Gibson also took charge on the mound, winning 19 times. That included the most important game of the season. Thanks to a late collapse by the Philadelphia Phillies, the Cardinals surged into first place in the last week of the season. They still

needed a win on the
final day to clinch the
pennant. Gibson relieved
starter Curt Simmons in
the fifth inning and shut
down the New York Mets,
and the offense rallied
for an 11–5 win. In the
World Series against the
Yankees, Gibson pitched
complete-game victories
in Games 5 and 7 as the
Cardinals won their first
title since 1946.

## FLYING HIGH

Cardinals third baseman Ken Boyer, *left*, congratulates Bob Gibson after the final out of the 1964 World Series.

The Cardinals returned
to the Fall Classic in 1967 with a retooled lineup, led by the
booming bat of Orlando Cepeda. The first baseman had already
made six All-Star teams with the San Francisco Giants before
arriving in a midseason trade in 1966. In 1967 he hit .325, led
the NL with 111 RBIs, and was the unanimous pick for the NL
MVP Award. Brock had an NL-best 52 stolen bases. Gibson
missed six weeks with a broken ankle. But 22-year-old Steve

**Lou Brock became baseball's all-time stolen base leader in 1977 and held the record until 1991.**

Carlton and 23-year-old Nelson Briles picked up the slack. They each won 14 games.

After posting 101 victories and winning the NL pennant by 10 1/2 games, St. Louis faced the Boston Red Sox in the World Series. Once again, Gibson came through under pressure, winning all three of his starts. That included a 7–2 win in

Game 7. Gibson even homered in the game as the Cardinals won a second title in four years. Brock also was brilliant, hitting .414 while scoring eight runs and stealing seven bases in the series.

A rule change to widen the strike zone in the 1960s favored pitchers. By 1968 hurlers were dominating. The season became known as "the Year of the Pitcher." But no one had a better year than Gibson. He finished 22–9. His earned-run average (ERA) of 1.12 was the lowest in baseball since 1914. In the AL, righty Denny McLain won 31 games for the Detroit Tigers. The two pitching stars collided in the World Series.

In Game 1, Gibson put on a show by striking out a World Series–record 17 batters. Brock tied a record with 13 hits and also stole seven bases. But it wasn't enough. The Tigers finally got to Gibson in Game 7. St. Louis's 4–1 loss dashed the city's hopes of back-to-back titles.

## SMALL BALL

The Cardinals had moved into Busch Memorial Stadium in 1966. But due to the summer heat and sharing the stadium with a football team, the grass field took a beating. In 1970 Busch became one of the first outdoor stadiums to replace its grass field with artificial turf. The hard surface created high hops off balls hit in front of home plate. In the outfield, line

Ozzie Smith's incredible defensive skills earned him 11 Gold Glove
Awards at shortstop during his time with the Cardinals.

drives skittered through the alleys all the way to the wall. And the Cardinals took advantage by building their roster around speedy players.

Brock was there already. He used his speed to break the single-season stolen base record with 118 in 1974. Brock retired in 1979 with 938 career steals, an MLB record at the time. Eventually, the Cardinals became known for playing "small ball." The team used stolen bases, bunts, and hit-and-run plays to put pressure on defenses.

That system paid off in 1982. That year the Cardinals hit a league-low 67 home runs. But they led the NL with 200 stolen bases. Left fielder Lonnie Smith swiped 68 to lead the way. A strong pitching staff was led by ace Joaquín Andújar and closer Bruce Sutter. The defense was led by Gold Glove winners Ozzie Smith at shortstop and Keith Hernandez at first base. The Cardinals made only 124 errors

## THE WIZARD

It would have made sense to call Ozzie Smith "the Wizard" even if he had a different first name. He performed magic on the field day in and day out for 15 seasons in St. Louis. Smith was an acrobat on the infield, using his quickness to track down grounders and a strong arm to throw out base runners. He won 13 straight Gold Gloves but was more known for his entrance to the field. Smith would often do a backflip when running out to his position before big games.

all year. St. Louis finished 92–70 and swept the Atlanta Braves in the NL Championship Series (NLCS).

That set up an interesting World Series matchup with the Milwaukee Brewers. Milwaukee was St. Louis's exact opposite. The team had hit 216 homers during the season. The Brewers pounded out 17 hits in a 10–0 Game 1 rout.

However, St. Louis bounced back, winning the next two in a series that would eventually reach seven games. In Game 7, St. Louis fell behind 3–1 in the sixth inning before rallying in the bottom half. Singles by Hernandez and George Hendrick brought in three runs to take the lead. The Cardinals added two more runs in the bottom of the eighth inning. Sutter pitched a perfect ninth to give St. Louis a 6–3 win and its first championship since 1967.

Manager Whitey Herzog led St. Louis back to the World Series twice more in the 1980s using the same formula. But St. Louis fell short in a pair of seven-game series, losing to the Kansas City Royals in 1985 and the Minnesota Twins in 1987. Small ball eventually fell out of favor, but the Cardinals soon showed they could also play power baseball.

The Cardinals race to celebrate with closer Bruce Sutter after the righty recorded the final out of the 1982 World Series.

# REACHING NEW HEIGHTS

After losing the 1987 World Series, the Cardinals drifted out of the playoffs until 1996. Two years later, they were on their way to a third-place finish. Yet the eyes of the baseball world were still on St. Louis—especially first baseman Mark McGwire.

The slugger had joined the Cardinals halfway through 1997 in a trade with the Oakland Athletics. He was already the A's all-time home run leader. Now he started crushing balls out of Busch Stadium.

Baseball's single-season mark of 61 home runs had stood since 1961 when it was set by Roger Maris. But as the summer of 1998 went on, it looked like that might fall. McGwire wasn't

Mark McGwire's 1998 chase of the single-season home run record captivated baseball fans all season long.

the only one launching homers. Both McGwire and Chicago Cubs right fielder Sammy Sosa were on pace to break the record during most of the season. The big question became which player would get there first.

The chase came at the perfect time for baseball. Just four years earlier, a strike had wiped out nearly half the season. It had even canceled the World Series. Angry fans stopped showing up at games. MLB needed excitement to bring those people back.

McGwire and Sosa did that with their home run show. But McGwire didn't just hit homers. He hit monster shots deep into the night sky.

## A RECORD FALLS

Both McGwire and Sosa entered September tied with 55 homers apiece. Then McGwire jumped ahead, starting the month with back-to-back two-homer games against the Florida Marlins. He hit number 60 on September 5. Adding to the drama, the Cubs came to town for a two-game series. McGwire tied the record in the first game, hitting his 61st homer of the year on his father's 61st birthday.

The crowds stood and cheered with every at-bat. Fans were still going wild for McGwire the next night when he stepped up in the fourth inning against Chicago's Steve Trachsel. On the

McGwire watches as his record-setting 62nd home run of the 1998 season leaves the ballpark in St. Louis.

first pitch, McGwire lined a hard shot down the left-field line. Unlike his usual majestic blasts, this one barely cleared the wall. At 341 feet (104 m), it was his shortest homer of the season. But it put him in the record books.

The Cubs infielders all congratulated McGwire as he trotted around the bases. He was so caught up in the moment that he nearly missed first base. When he reached home plate, McGwire lifted his son into the air before his teammates mobbed him. Maris was no longer living, but his family was on hand to congratulate McGwire. Sosa even ran in from right field to wrap McGwire in a bear hug.

However, the race wasn't over. Sosa bashed four homers in three games to give him 62 on September 13. With two games to play, the sluggers were tied at 66. Then McGwire hit four homers over the last two games while Sosa came up empty. The Cardinals' first baseman had set the new record with 70.

McGwire stayed with the Cardinals for three more seasons and hit 126 more homers. Eventually it came out that both players were using performance-enhancing drugs (PEDs). The new information tainted the home run chase. But it never removed the memories of the Summer of '98.

## A NEW ERA

McGwire shared the field with a sensational rookie during his final summer in St. Louis. Albert Pujols was not a big-time prospect. He was a 13th-round pick in the 1999 draft. But he made the team in 2001 and immediately became a star. By the end of the year, he'd become just the fourth rookie in MLB history to hit .300 with at least 30 home runs, 100 runs scored, and 100 RBIs.

It was just a sign of things to come. Fans began calling Pujols "the Machine" because he was so consistent. In his first 10 MLB seasons, he averaged 41 homers, 123 RBIs, and a .331

In 2022 Albert Pujols joined Hank Aaron as the only players with 3,000 career hits and 700 career home runs.

batting average. Pujols hit .359 to win the MLB batting title in 2003. By 2010 he had won two NL home run crowns and was a three-time NL MVP.

Even better, the Cardinals were winning again. They reached the playoffs seven times in Pujols's first 11 seasons. In 2004 they won 105 games but were swept by a red-hot Boston Red Sox team in the World Series. Two years later, the Cardinals made a surprise return to the Fall Classic. They had won only 83 games, but that was enough to take first place in a weak NL Central. Then they got on a roll, beating the New York Mets in a thrilling seven-game NLCS. The Cardinals beat the Tigers in five games. Young catcher Yadier Molina hit .412, and rookie reliever Adam Wainwright posted a win and a save.

Pujols was in the final year of his contract in 2011. He helped the Cardinals slip into the playoffs, as they won the NL wild card by one game. St. Louis then upset the Philadelphia Phillies and Milwaukee Brewers to reach the World Series. Their opponents, the Texas Rangers, were battle-tested after a tough run through the AL playoffs. And the series was nothing short of epic.

## PUJOLS POWER

**Though he was later overshadowed by David Freese's heroics, Albert Pujols accomplished a rare feat in Game 3 of the 2011 World Series. The slugger hit three home runs in a 16–7 St. Louis win. In doing so, he joined Babe Ruth and Reggie Jackson as the only players ever to hit three homers in a World Series game.**

## HOMETOWN MAGIC

The Rangers held a 3–2 lead as the series moved back to St. Louis for a memorable Game 6. In a slugfest, the Rangers took a 7–5 lead into the bottom of the ninth inning. With two outs and two runners on base, Cardinals third baseman David Freese came to the plate.

David Freese, *center*, is surrounded by teammates at home plate after his walk-off home run in Game 6 of the 2011 World Series.

The St. Louis native drove a pitch to right field for a two-run triple that tied the game and saved the Cardinals' season.

Texas jumped back ahead with a two-run homer in the 10th inning. Again the Cardinals fought their way back, tying the game on Lance Berkman's two-out RBI single. Freese came back up in the bottom of the 11th with the game tied 10–10. On a 3–2 pitch, he blasted a walk-off home run to center field to force Game 7.

The Rangers jumped to a 2–0 lead in the first inning of Game 7. But Freese erased it with a two-run double in the bottom half. From there, St. Louis ace Chris Carpenter calmed down to pitch six innings. Left fielder Allen Craig's third-inning home run put St. Louis ahead to stay. The 6–2 win gave the Cardinals a total of 11 World Series titles. That was second only to the New York Yankees.

## MOVING ON

After that series, two longtime Cardinals left. Manager Tony La Russa stepped down after 16 years in charge. And Pujols broke St. Louis hearts by signing a 10-year contract with the Los Angeles Angels.

Despite the losses, the Cardinals carried on. They reached the playoffs seven times in the next 10 years. In Pujols's absence, Wainwright and Molina became the team's leaders. Wainwright was a consistent Cy Young contender who won at least 19 games four times. Molina was a solid hitter and the best defensive catcher in the league. By 2022 only Stan Musial and Lou Brock had played more games as a Cardinal than the veteran catcher.

The Cardinals have always developed their own players well. But two of the team's current stars came from outside the organization. First baseman Paul Goldschmidt joined in 2019 and hit 34 home runs his first season. Third baseman Nolan Arenado joined up in 2021 after a trade with the Colorado Rockies. He hit 34 home runs and won his ninth straight Gold Glove.

In 2022 a 42-year-old Pujols came home to play one more season with Wainwright and Molina. On September 23, the slugger homered twice against the Los Angeles Dodgers. The second shot was the 700th of his career. He became just the fourth player to reach that historic milestone. And he did it playing for one of baseball's most storied franchises.

Nolan Arenado had a team-high 105 RBIs during his first season with the Cardinals in 2021.

**1882**

The St. Louis Brown Stockings begin play in the American Association.

**1892**

The team, now called the Browns, joins the National League.

**1900**

After spending one season as the Perfectos, the team changes its name to the Cardinals.

**1925**

Rogers Hornsby wins his second NL Triple Crown and takes over as manager.

**1926**

The Cardinals win their first World Series, defeating the New York Yankees in seven games.

**1931**

Behind NL MVP Frankie Frisch, the Cardinals defeat the Philadelphia Athletics in seven games to win the World Series.

**1934**

The Dean brothers and the rest of the Gashouse Gang knock off the Detroit Tigers in a thrilling seven-game World Series.

**1946**

The Cardinals win Game 7 of the World Series when "Slaughter's Mad Dash" beats the Boston Red Sox.

**1963**

Stan Musial retires with an NL-record 3,630 hits.

## 1964

Led by ace pitcher Bob Gibson and NL MVP Ken Boyer, the Cardinals defeat the Yankees in the World Series.

## 1967

Gibson pitches the Cardinals to another title, winning three games against the Red Sox in the Fall Classic.

## 1974

Lou Brock sets an NL single-season record with 118 stolen bases.

## 1982

Despite hitting only 67 home runs all season, the Cardinals win the World Series over the Milwaukee Brewers.

## 1998

Mark McGwire breaks Roger Maris's single-season record when he finishes the season with 70 homers.

## 2006

The Cardinals make a surprise run to the World Series, where they beat the Tigers in five games.

## 2011

David Freese's Game 6 heroics help the Cardinals defeat the Texas Rangers to win the World Series.

## 2022

Albert Pujols returns to the Cardinals after 10 years away, and he hits his 700th career home run in September.

# TEAM FACTS

## FRANCHISE HISTORY

St. Louis Brown Stockings
(1882)
St. Louis Browns (1883–98)
St. Louis Perfectos (1899)
St. Louis Cardinals (1900– )

## WORLD SERIES CHAMPIONSHIPS

1926, 1931, 1934, 1942, 1944,
1946, 1964, 1967, 1982,
2006, 2011

## KEY PLAYERS

Ken Boyer (1955–65)
Lou Brock (1964–79)
Dizzy Dean (1930, 1932–37)
Curt Flood (1958–69)
Frankie Frisch (1927–37)
Bob Gibson (1959–75)
Rogers Hornsby
(1915–26, 1933)
Joe Medwick (1932–40,
1947–48)
Yadier Molina (2004–22 )
Stan Musial (1941–44, 1946–63)

Albert Pujols (2001–11, 2022)
Ted Simmons (1968–80)
Enos Slaughter (1938–42,
1946–53)
Ozzie Smith (1982–96)
Adam Wainwright (2005– )

## KEY MANAGERS

Whitey Herzog (1980–90)
Tony La Russa (1996–2011)
Red Schoendienst (1965–76,
1980, 1990)

## HOME STADIUMS

Sportsman's Park II (1882–91)
Robison Field (1892–1920)
Also known as:
Union Park (1892–97)
League Park (1898)
Sportsman's Park III (1920–52)
Also known as:
Busch Stadium (1953–65)
Busch Stadium II (1966–2005)
Busch Stadium III (2006– )

## GOING DEEP

On May 2, 1954, Stan Musial hit a record five home runs in a doubleheader against the New York Giants. Two of them came against future Hall of Famer Hoyt Wilhelm.

## HOME AND AWAY

Musial retired with 3,630 hits. Amazingly, he hit exactly the same number at home (1,815) as on the road.

## SPEED MERCHANT

Vince Coleman stole 110 bases as a rookie in 1985. Then he stole 107 bases the next year to become the first player ever to steal more than 100 bases in each of his first two seasons. He extended the streak to three years with 109 steals in 1987.

## SECRET WEAPON

St. Louis utility man José Oquendo played all nine positions at some point during the 1988 season. Oquendo's versatility earned him the nickname "the Secret Weapon" from manager Whitey Herzog. Oquendo even made a pitching appearance that year, taking the mound in a 19-inning game against the Atlanta Braves on May 14.

# GLOSSARY

**ace**

A team's best starting pitcher.

**bullpen**

The area of a baseball field where relief pitchers warm up; also used to refer to a team's relievers as a group.

**closer**

A pitcher who comes in at the end of the game to secure a win for his team.

**farm system**

In baseball, all the minor league teams that feed players to one major league team.

**franchise**

A sports organization, including the top-level team and all minor league affiliates.

**free agent**

A player whose rights are not owned by any team.

**no-hitter**

A complete game in which a team does not allow any hits.

**pennant**

Another name for a league championship; in MLB, it refers to winning either the American or National League.

**save**

When a relief pitcher comes into a close game and preserves a win.

**shutout**

A complete game in which a team allows no runs.

# MORE INFORMATION

## BOOKS

Flynn, Brendan. *The MLB Encyclopedia*. Minneapolis, MN: Abdo Publishing, 2022.

Gitlin, Marty. *Baseball: Underdog Stories*. Minneapolis, MN: Abdo Publishing, 2019.

Hustad, Douglas. *Innovations in Baseball*. Minneapolis, MN: Abdo Publishing, 2021.

## ONLINE RESOURCES

To learn more about the St. Louis Cardinals, please visit **abdobooklinks.com** or scan this QR code. These links are routinely monitored and updated to provide the most current information available.

## ABOUT THE AUTHOR

Patrick Donnelly is a freelance writer who lives in Minneapolis, Minnesota. He has covered Major League Baseball for more than 20 years.